DIGITAL PHOTOGRAPHY

PORTRAIT PHOTOGRAPHY

By John Hamilton

Abdo & Daughters
An imprint of Abdo Publishing | abdopublishing.com

abdopublishing.com

Published by Abdo Publishing, a division of ABDO, PO Box 398166, Minneapolis, Minnesota 55439. Copyright © 2019 by Abdo Consulting Group, Inc. International copyrights reserved in all countries. No part of this book may be reproduced in any form without written permission from the publisher. Abdo & Daughters™ is a trademark and logo of Abdo Publishing.

Printed in the United States of America, North Mankato, Minnesota.
082018
092018

Editor: Sue Hamilton
Copy Editor: Bridget O'Brien
Graphic Design: Sue Hamilton
Cover Design: Candice Keimig and Pakou Moua
Cover Photos: John Hamilton & iStock
Interior Images: Eastman-Kodak-pg 8 (top); Fujifilm North America-pg 13; iStock-pgs 7, 11, 12, 14, 15, 18 (top), 19, 20 (top), 21, 22, 23 (top), 24, 25, 26, 28, 29, 30, 31, 32, 34, 35, 36-37, 38, 39, 40, 41, 42, 44 & 45 (top); John Hamilton-pgs 4-5, 16, 17 (top), 18 (bottom), 27, 33 & 43; Nikon USA-pgs 9 (inset), 10, 14 (inset), 15 (inset), 16 (inset), 17 (inset) & 20 (bottom); Shutterstock-pgs 6, 8 (bottom), 9, 17 (bottom) & 23 (bottom); U.S. Copyright Office-pg 45 (bottom).

Library of Congress Control Number: 2017963905
Publisher's Cataloging-in-Publication Data
Names: Hamilton, John, author.
Title: Portrait photography / by John Hamilton.
Description: Minneapolis, Minnesota : Abdo Publishing, 2019. | Series: Digital photography | Includes online resources and index.
Identifiers: ISBN 9781532115899 (lib.bdg.) | ISBN 9781532156823 (ebook)
Subjects: LCSH: Portrait photography--Juvenile literature. | Photography--Technique--Juvenile literature. | Photography--Digital techniques--Juvenile literature.
Classification: DDC 778.92--dc23

CONTENTS

THE ART OF PORTRAITS

Great portrait photographers are masters of many skills. Learning about cameras and lenses and lighting is important. But developing people skills is vital. The most striking part of a great portrait is how it brings out a subject's personality.

Why you take a picture of somebody is just as important as how. A portrait is more than just a snapshot. As a photographer, you are trying to show what makes a person tick. How do you bring out the best, or worst, of your subject? Will you try to hide certain traits? Will your lighting and lens choices flatter the subject? How does the subject behave differently in front of the camera, and how do you make them relax to capture their true personality as you see it?

GAIN A SUBJECT'S TRUST BY TALKING

This portrait of Lyle Glass, of Medora, North Dakota, was taken on a park bench in the shade. Reflected light from the sidewalk filled in the shadows. After chatting for a few minutes, the photographer asked permission to take the cowboy's portrait. He continued talking as he was shooting. He discovered that when Cowboy Lyle wasn't wrangling horses, he played Theodore Roosevelt in the famous Medora Musical, making nearly 3,000 appearances.

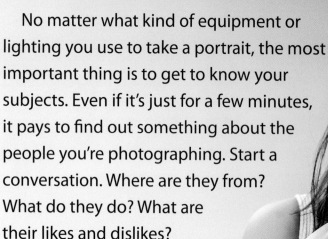

No matter what kind of equipment or lighting you use to take a portrait, the most important thing is to get to know your subjects. Even if it's just for a few minutes, it pays to find out something about the people you're photographing. Start a conversation. Where are they from? What do they do? What are their likes and dislikes?

The simple act of talking with someone lowers their guard. When you start taking photos, that human connection translates into expressions that are more genuine. Instead of forced smiles, you capture honest happiness. Instead of photographing zombie stares, you'll find earnest thought, or joy, or sadness. As a portrait photographer, it's your job to find the real person behind the public mask most people wear. Getting to know your subjects is the best way to start.

Sometimes, you only have a few minutes or less to take a good portrait. How do you get people to lower their guard? One trick is to have them jump in place and take a picture of them in mid-air. Or have them loudly repeat a nonsensical phrase. If there are two or more people in the picture, have one tug another's ear. All of these tricks will bring out a genuine emotional reaction immediately afterwards (usually a genuine smile). Have your camera ready to capture the moment.

CAMERAS

Digital photography captures a scene when light passes through a lens and is focused onto an image sensor. The sensor converts the light into digital form. It is then stored as a file that can be transferred to a computer for later processing. The first portable digital camera was made by Eastman Kodak in 1975. It weighed eight pounds (3.6 kg) and shot only in black-and-white. Digital cameras as we know them today first became popular in the 1990s and early 2000s.

The first portable digital camera was made by Steven Sasson for Eastman Kodak in 1975.

Most portrait photography today is done digitally because of the many advantages over film. One of the best parts is seeing your photos right away so you can change settings if needed. Also, you can take hundreds of shots on a single memory card. That reduces the chance of missing a great shot because you're busy changing a low-capacity film cartridge.

Digital cameras allow you to check your photos and change settings if needed.

With a DSLR (Digital Single Lens Reflex) camera, you can look through the viewfinder or use the camera's screen display to see exactly what you're shooting.

Most professional portrait photographers today use DSLR (Digital Single Lens Reflex) cameras. With a DSLR, you actually peer through the camera lens so you can see exactly what you're shooting. Angle of view and sharpness are determined by the lens. DSLR lenses are "interchangeable," which means you can change one lens for another depending on your creative needs.

When light travels inside the DSLR, it is diverted by a mirror into a glass prism. It directs the light into the viewfinder. When you press the shutter release button, this "reflex" mirror flips up and the shutter behind it opens. Light strikes the image processor. After the exposure, the shutter closes, and the mirror flips back down.

The image sensor inside the camera has millions of light-capturing pixels that record an image. The greater the number of pixels, the higher the resolution of the picture. A 20-megapixel (20-million-pixel) sensor almost always has a better resolution than a 10-megapixel sensor. Modern DSLR sensors usually come equipped with at least 16 to 24 megapixels. The size of the image sensor is also important. The large sensors in many DSLRs produce the most detailed pictures, and they can capture images in low light without too much digital noise ruining the scene.

The inside workings of a DSLR camera.

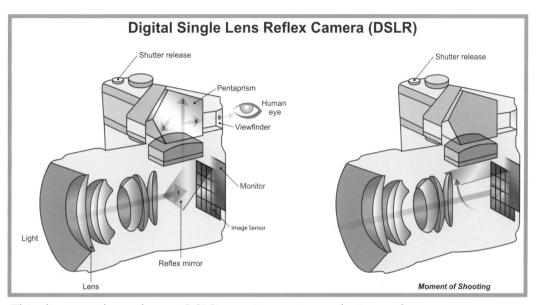

Digital Single Lens Reflex Camera (DSLR)

Shutter release

Pentaprism

Human eye

Viewfinder

Monitor

Image Sensor

Light

Reflex mirror

Lens

Shutter release

Moment of Shooting

This diagram shows how a DSLR camera creates a photograph.

8 TIPS FOR CARING FOR YOUR CAMERA

1. Use an air blower and microfiber cloth to clean your camera regularly.
2. Use a strap when carrying your camera.
3. When not in use, keep the camera safe in a bag or case.
4. Many photographers put a UV or skylight filter on the front of their lenses. These block ultraviolet rays from the Sun (which degrade image quality) and protect your expensive lenses from dust or scratches.
5. Make sure you always have spare batteries.
6. Keep your camera out of the rain.
7. Keep your camera out of hot cars.
8. Never leave your camera unattended.

Cell phones are commonly used as both a primary and a backup camera. Most cell phones have a complicated lens arrangement. This has helped improve their photo quality greatly in recent years.

There is an old saying that the best camera is the one you have on you. For many people, that means a cell phone. The image quality of most cell phones has greatly improved in recent years. Most professional photographers carry one as a backup in case their DSLRs are not handy when a photo opportunity arises. Cell phones automatically focus and adjust exposure. Many allow you to manually override these settings for creative effects. Some even have dual lenses that let you simulate a shallow depth of field. This throws the background out of focus while keeping the subject sharp for a pleasing portrait effect.

Cell phone cameras do have disadvantages. It usually takes longer to set up a shot than with a DSLR. Adjusting exposure with an app and attaching a clip-on lens can be awkward. In addition, cell phone cameras are tricky in low-light situations. Be sure to hold it steady, or even use a tripod with a special mount, to avoid blurry photos.

Mirrorless cameras are becoming more popular each year. Like DSLRs, different lenses can be mounted on most of them (some have fixed lenses). However, there is no mirror or glass prism. This makes mirrorless cameras lightweight and quiet to shoot. Yet, they have excellent image quality, even in low light.

If you are a beginner, don't worry too much about which camera to buy. Think about what you want to do with it and which features are important to you. Amazing images can be taken with almost all digital cameras sold today. The truth is, it's the creative mind behind the camera that matters most.

A mirrorless camera produced by Fujifilm. This type of camera is lightweight and quiet to shoot, yet produces excellent image quality, even in low light.

LENSES

Just as important as your camera are the lenses you use. They determine the "field of view" of your scene. A wide-angle lens shows more of the surrounding area. A telephoto lens captures just a small part, which is why everything looks magnified.

A lens's field of view is measured in millimeters. A "normal" field of view captured by a full-frame image sensor is about 50mm. That is about the same as what you perceive with your eyes. Common wide-angle lenses are about 24mm to 35mm. Super-wide lenses start at about 10mm. Below that are fisheye lenses, which are used for special effects because of their distortion.

A 10mm fisheye lens causes distortion that bends straight lines.

A 24mm wide-angle lens captures the portrait subject and the surrounding area.

Most portrait photographers own at least one wide-angle lens. (Wide-angle zooms are a popular choice.) These lenses make it easier to photograph large groups of people. They work well in low light. They also have a tremendous range of focus, or "depth of field." That makes them easier to use for selfies. Despite these advantages, wide-angle lenses aren't often used for portraits. The distortion they create is usually unflattering.

FILTERS

The most common lens filters used by portrait photographers are clear UV (ultraviolet) filters. Most are round and screw onto the front of a lens. They have a coating that blocks invisible ultraviolet light waves, which can reduce picture clarity. More importantly, UV filters protect expensive lenses from smears, scratches, or even shattering. Buy only from reputable stores. Cheap UV filters can affect image sharpness.

A 24-70mm zoom can capture small groups in their environment.

A 50mm lens, which is included in many camera starter kits, is fine when you need to capture a full-length portrait of a person. It can also be handy for group shots. Some photographers carry a zoom lens that includes a range of medium focal lengths, such as a 24-70mm zoom.

However, when you shoot a close-up portrait with a 50mm lens, faces begin to look distorted and stretched. That's definitely not the look you want for your portrait photos. Moderate telephotos, on the other hand, create a compression effect in the subject. Noses and other facial features seem to flatten out slightly. It creates a very flattering look that most people like. Long lenses also make it easier to shoot with a shallow depth of field, which blurs distracting backgrounds.

A 70-210mm zoom contains excellent portrait focal lengths, 85mm to 105mm.

There is no "best" lens for portraits. However, many professional photographers prefer to shoot in the moderate telephoto range, from about 85mm to 105mm. A 70-210mm zoom lens covers this entire range, plus it gives a little extra "reach" when needed.

LENS HOODS

LENS HOOD →

Lens hoods are plastic (usually) extensions that fit onto the front of your lens. They keep Sun flare from washing out your photos. They can also protect your expensive lens's front glass element from bumps and scratches.

EXPOSURE

Exposure is the amount of light that strikes the camera's image sensor. Three settings determine the "correct" exposure. They include ISO, shutter speed, and aperture. All three work together.

A camera's shutter-speed dial.

ISO is the image sensor's sensitivity to light. If you double the ISO, you make the sensor twice as sensitive. However, more digital noise is then created. The lower the ISO, the better the quality. For example, when shooting in bright sunlight, you would normally set an ISO of 100 or 200. However, in dim scenes, you might increase it to 800. Otherwise, your exposures would be so long that you couldn't hold your camera steady enough to avoid blurring (camera shake). Blurring can also occur if your subject moves during long exposures.

This photograph shows noticeable camera shake. It is very apparent in the subjects' eyes and hair.

In this image the shutter speed was increased from 1/125 to 1/250 second. The subjects are much sharper.

Choosing the right exposure for a portrait is a balance between areas of light and dark (tone) and focus (depth of field). These are controlled by shutter speed and aperture.

Shutter speed is the length of time the camera's shutter opens to let light strike the image sensor. It is measured in seconds (usually a fraction of a second). Each setting is twice as long, or half as short, as the setting next to it. Shutter speeds must be fairly fast to avoid camera shake, usually in the range of 1/125 to 1/250 second. Wide-angle lenses can be used with slower shutter speeds.

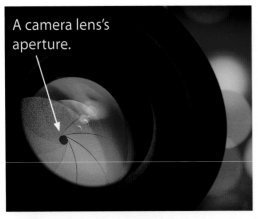

A camera lens's aperture.

Lenses have apertures, or holes, in the back where they are mounted to the camera. Apertures can be adjusted much like the irises in your eyes. They are measured in "f-stops." The smaller the f-stop number, the more light is allowed into the camera.

The important thing to remember is that if you increase one setting, such as shutter speed, then you must reduce the other setting (aperture) in order to get back to your original exposure.

When you are starting out, it's okay to put your camera on automatic. DSLRs have a setting on the exposure dial called "P," which stands for program mode. Modern cameras are like small computers. They examine the scene and figure out the math for you. The camera will pick a shutter speed and aperture combination. This will allow you to concentrate on other things, like focus and composition.

The exposure dial is set at "P" for program mode.

Large Depth of Field-Sharp Overall

Portraits with a lot of depth of field produce sharp overall subjects. Try using f-stops from f/11 to f/16.

Shallow Depth of Field-Eyes Sharp

For a shallow depth of field effect, try f/2.8 to f/4. Get close to your subject and focus on the eye nearest the camera.

As you get more practice taking pictures, you'll soon want to control these settings yourself in creative ways. For example, controlling the aperture also controls the amount of depth of field in your scene. That means you have control over what is in sharp focus.

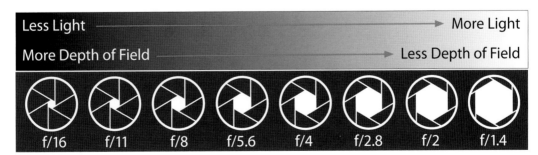

Typical lens f-stop settings.

GETTING A STEADY SHOT

When you handhold your camera, pictures can get blurry during long exposures. This is especially true when light levels are dim, such as at dusk, or in a wooded park or dark alley. When you take portraits in natural light, you might need extra support to avoid camera shake.

If there's one piece of equipment every photographer should own, it's a sturdy tripod. You simply cannot handhold your camera in dim light and expect sharp results, especially with a telephoto lens. You can raise your camera's ISO to make it more sensitive to light, but that reduces quality by increasing digital noise.

To properly handhold your camera, make sure your elbows are tucked in near your body. The camera should rest in the palm of your hand. Gently squeeze the shutter release. Don't stab at it with your finger. These steps will help you get a steady shot.

Tripods come in many shapes and sizes, and some can be very expensive. In general, the best tripods are heavy (to give your camera a

Tripods give your camera a solid platform.

solid platform), made of metal or carbon fiber, and have adjustable-length tubular legs.

If you shoot in a studio using artificial light, you might not need to use a tripod. Flash and continuous studio lights (either incandescent, fluorescent, or LED) usually provide enough illumination to handhold your camera without worrying about camera shake. Many studio photographers like to handhold their camera so they can move around the set more easily. Others prefer using a tripod. Once the camera is set up, they can concentrate on directing the subject.

BEST SHUTTER SPEED FOR HANDHOLDING THE CAMERA

If you're handholding your camera, how do you know if the shutter speed is fast enough to create a sharp image? The rule of thumb is to shoot at a shutter speed higher than the reciprocal of the focal length of your lens. In other words, if you're shooting with a 200mm lens, you'll need a shutter speed of at least 1/200 second in order to get a sharp picture. If you're shooting with a wide-angle 24mm lens, you can go all the way down to 1/24 second. If you set your camera to "Program" or "Auto," it will calculate this for you.

COMPOSITION

Composition is where creative photographers get their chance to shine. You don't need fancy equipment or exotic locations to make stunning images. Composition is all about arranging the scene in your viewfinder in the best way to tell your story.

Good composition uses many artistic elements. They include color, contrast, texture, framing, and natural lines, all of which lead the viewer's eye to your subject. One of the most important things is to reduce clutter in your scene, and the best way to do that is to fill the frame with your subject. Be aware of empty space around your subject and get closer if you can.

Backgrounds can help or hurt your composition. Sometimes a busy background will give context to your scene. Other times, it distracts from the person you're photographing. Before taking a photo, check to be sure things like poles or pillars aren't growing out of the head of your subjects. Large apertures, such as f/2.8 on some lenses, will blur the background, hiding much of the clutter.

THE RULE OF THIRDS

Many portraits have their subjects in the center of the photograph. There is nothing wrong with this, especially if you're filling the frame with a person's face. Sometimes, however, you may want to be more creative with your compositions, especially if you're including the background. The "rule of thirds" is a way of dividing the viewfinder into three horizontal parts and three vertical parts. Instead of a "rule," think of it as a helpful guideline. Oftentimes, putting your subject off-center makes the composition more pleasing and interesting.

KINDS OF PORTRAITS

A good portrait tells a story. This can be a difficult thing to do with just one photo, a single moment frozen in time. To tell a person's story, sometimes it takes more than simply having them pose and smile for the camera. There are other techniques in the photographer's toolbox that are often used to capture a person's personality.

Posed photos are what people usually think of when they hear the word portrait. The photographer directs the subjects, telling them where to stand or sit, what to wear, and whether to smile or have a serious expression. Almost everything is controlled from the start.

POSED PORTRAIT

A posed portrait lets the subject and photographer plan out what will be worn, where the portrait will be taken, and what kind of expression the person will have.

CAMERA-AWARE PORTRAIT

CANDID PORTRAIT

A camera-aware portrait is more casual. These kinds of photos are not usually arranged in advance. They happen during some kind of event or activity. The subject looks into the lens, but isn't being directed by the photographer.

A candid portrait is when the subject ignores or isn't aware of the photographer. Candid portraits capture a subject's life in some way. These "slice of life" moments can be very effective storytelling tools. They have their roots in photojournalism.

ENVIRONMENTAL PORTRAITS

One good way to tell someone's story is to take their portrait surrounded by items in their everyday life. Environmental portraits reveal someone's character in a different way than a basic portrait that simply records their face. These kinds of photographs also show how people work, relax, and play. In the hands of a skilled photographer, an environmental portrait can tell us much about a subject's life.

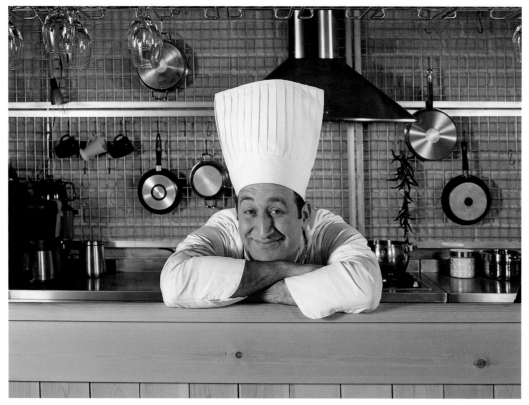

A chef comfortable in his kitchen makes for a good environmental portrait.

A carpenter looks relaxed and happy in his workshop portrait.

To successfully shoot subjects in their workplace or home environment, you have to help them relax. They'll be on their home turf instead of an intimidating photo studio, so getting them to loosen up isn't usually too hard. The main thing is to listen to what they have to say. What is their favorite thing about their job or hobby? What do they get the most excited talking about? If you're listening, you'll get good clues to the kind of photo your subject wants. Include your subject in your creative ideas. They'll be more relaxed if they feel like they're a part of creating their own portrait.

PHOTOGRAPHING CHILDREN

The trouble with many children's portraits is that they're shot from too high up. Most adults take pictures of kids while standing, so the subjects appear small. Even if you fill the frame when shooting from above, it results in an odd perspective. The kids are looking up at the camera, with their heads disproportionately larger than their bodies because of the angle. That gives them a kind of cartoony appearance.

Photos of kids looking up at the camera gives them a funny, cartoony appearance.

To really photograph young children and show them as the real people they are, get down to their level. Shoot on your knees or sit

on the floor so that the camera is at or below their head level. In our day-to-day lives, most grown-ups don't see kids from this perspective. A child's portrait taken at this lower viewpoint gives it added impact.

The best kid photos are taken with the photographer at their level or lower, looking up at them. It helps to take photos at a place where they are comfortable, such as at a playground or their home.

Use sports equipment or a special toy to bring out a child's real personality. These props also help them feel less shy and nervous during a photo shoot.

To keep children from being too shy or distracted by the camera, be sure to talk to them as you're shooting. You can also use toys or props. Try to make the session fun to bring out their real personalities.

WORKING WITH NATURAL LIGHT

Making portraits with natural light simply means using the Sun as your main illumination. Depending on the time of day, natural light may be all you need to create a professional-quality portrait. During early morning or at dusk, the Sun gives off a wonderful, warm light. If clouds cover the Sun, the quality of light is diffused. There are fewer shadows, and the contrast between light and dark decreases, which makes for pleasing-looking portraits.

The natural light at sunrise or sunset gives portraits a wonderful, warm glow.

Hard Light

Soft Light

OPEN SHADE

During the light of the midday Sun, people's skin becomes shiny in portraits. Hot spots show up as featureless white blobs. Harsh shadows can create inky blotches under the eyes. Instead of shooting in direct sunlight, move your subject to a shady spot that blocks the Sun, such as under a tree or a roof awning. This "open shade" softens and diffuses the hard light of the Sun. Open your lens up wide, to f/2.8 for example. This will give you a fast shutter speed, allowing you to handhold without camera shake. It will also throw the background out of focus. This separation between the background and the sharp foreground will make your subject the center of attention.

BACKLIGHTING

Backlighting means putting your light source—the Sun—directly behind your portrait subject. The Sun itself doesn't necessarily have to appear in the frame, although that can result in very dramatic and trendy photos. Backlighting creates a halo around your subject, and hair seems to glow.

If you just take a quick picture with the Sun behind your subject, you'll get a silhouette. For portraits, first use your camera's meter and aim at your subject's face. That tells the camera to expose for your subject, and not the bright background. Lock in the exposure (see your camera's manual for instructions) and start shooting. It may take a few tries, but the results make it worth the effort.

WINDOW LIGHT

Photographing with natural lights doesn't mean you always have to shoot outdoors. One of the best tools at a photographer's disposal is sunlight pouring in from a large window. The light can be very directional and dramatic, or soft and diffused. For contrasty hard light, have your subject stand next to the window, maybe gazing outside as if in deep thought. You stand directly next to your subject, to their right or left.

For a softer look you need to diffuse the light streaming through the window. Attach a white bed sheet, or even a frosted vinyl shower curtain, over the window. That diffuses the light, spreading it out to softly wrap around your portrait subject.

POSING

Most of your portrait subjects may feel uncomfortable at first. They are not trained to pose and look their best. Your job is to help them feel comfortable and to follow your directions in a fun way. You want them to appear to be acting naturally, not posed. Sometimes it's best to let your subjects act in their own natural way, to "do their own thing." Make your conversations with them lighthearted to keep them from feeling self-conscious.

Try directing your subjects instead of posing them. Give them emotions to play, or roles to act out. Say things like, "Pretend you're the king of England," or "How would you look if you just won the lottery?" Shoot while they're acting out, and also immediately afterward to catch unguarded moments. If you must pose someone (for example, you want them to place their hands in a certain way), instead of saying left or right, use your hands to signal which way to move. It's awkward when you say, "Move a bit to the left. No, *my* left!" Just point. That'll keep your subject from feeling dumb and self-conscious.

Use motion to catch candid moments. Have your subjects shake out their hair, or walk forward a few steps. Capturing them in mid-motion creates an interesting shot, and makes the subject seem unposed.

Keep your subjects involved in the shoot. Stop frequently to show them their photos on the camera's LED screen. People love seeing how they look in pictures. Showing them your work-in-progress will boost their enthusiasm and give them a better idea of how you want them to pose.

LIGHTING EQUIPMENT

Sometimes sunlight isn't available, or you want more control when lighting your portrait subjects. There are many tools to create and control artificial light. Flash units, also called strobes, create a brief burst of light. They range from large, powerful units used in professional photo studios, to small strobes (often called speedlights) that can be handheld, mounted to a stand, or attached to a hotshoe bracket on top of the camera.

Flash/Strobe

When fired directly on top of the camera, strobes give off an even, harsh light. They can also cause the dreaded red-eye effect in your subjects. For best results, use one or more wireless-controlled flash units off-camera to sculpt the light for creative effects. Entire books and websites are devoted to this subject. They include excellent tutorials by professional photographers such as Scott Kelby, Joe McNally, and David Hobby.

Continuous Studio Lights

CONTINUOUS LIGHT

Continuous photographic lights provide a steady stream of illumination. Their biggest advantage is that you can see exactly the effect you want before you press the shutter button. However, they're not as portable as small flash units, and they can heat up a small studio very quickly. But unlike strobes, continuous lights can double as lights used for video production.

Continuous lights are often called studio lights, or hot lights. They mainly use bright tungsten or fluorescent bulbs. In recent years, LED lights have become more popular. They are lightweight, use less energy, and don't give off as much heat.

Diffuser

Reflector

A combination of light modifiers, such as a reflector and a diffuser, help photographers control how a subject is illuminated.

LIGHT MODIFIERS

A reflector can be an expensive panel you buy in a camera store, or it can be a simple piece of white cardboard you make yourself. You use it to reflect light onto the shady side of a portrait subject's face. Simply place or hold the reflector near the front of your subject's head and adjust its position to fill in the shadows.

Diffusers are semi-transparent sheets of material. They spread, or "diffuse," hard directional light. You place diffusers between the subject and the Sun, a strobe, or other artificial light source. Diffusers create a soft, glowing effect that is very pleasing for portraits. You can make them yourself using materials such as white bed sheets or frosted shower curtains.

Umbrella

Softboxes

Photographic umbrellas are inexpensive light modifying tools. They are attached to stands along with a strobe or continuous light source. The light bounces off the umbrella's reflective surface and spreads out. The resulting light has an even quality that fills in shadows. It works especially well when placed very close to the subject.

Softboxes are similar to umbrellas, but the strobe or continuous light source is contained inside a fabric box. Light escapes through a diffusion panel on one side. Soft boxes create a narrower beam of light than umbrellas. That makes the soft light more controllable. However, they are more expensive and difficult to set up.

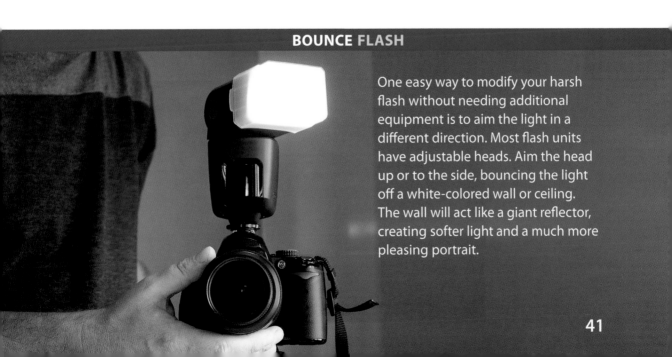

BOUNCE FLASH

One easy way to modify your harsh flash without needing additional equipment is to aim the light in a different direction. Most flash units have adjustable heads. Aim the head up or to the side, bouncing the light off a white-colored wall or ceiling. The wall will act like a giant reflector, creating softer light and a much more pleasing portrait.

THE DIGITAL DARKROOM

Photos taken with modern cameras are usually well exposed and in focus, but there's always room for improvement. That's where the digital darkroom comes in. Fixing a photo's range of tones (its light and dark pixels) can improve it dramatically. Color balance, sharpening, and cropping are also common enhancements. These are all easy to perform with modern digital photo software, such as Photoshop, Lightroom, or GIMP. There are even inexpensive apps for cell phones that let you experiment with your photos.

Image editing software can be difficult to learn, but it is a fun way to improve your photos. Use the software's help menus, or search for online video instructions. Everyone was a beginner once, and many generous photographers are happy to share their skills.

Postproduction work can dramatically enhance a photo.

The left photo above is before image enhancement. In Photoshop, the first task was to fix the exposure and contrast. Yellow was added to counter the blue cast, common on cloudy days. Color vibrance was boosted, and then a vignette circled the image to draw the viewer's eye toward the center of the frame.

BACKING UP YOUR PHOTOS

Make copies of your digital images. Keep them safe on at least two storage devices. All hard drives will fail eventually. Without a backup, your photos will vanish, representing many months, perhaps years, of hard work.

In most professional studios, photos are backed up on several different devices. In addition to the hard drive on your main computer, use backup software every day to automatically copy all your photos onto a portable hard drive. These small devices get cheaper every year, with bigger capacities. Every few days or weeks, swap out the external drive with one that you might keep in a safe deposit box at your bank. This strategy is called having an off-site backup. If disaster strikes, such as your house burning down or washing away in a flood, your work will remain safe.

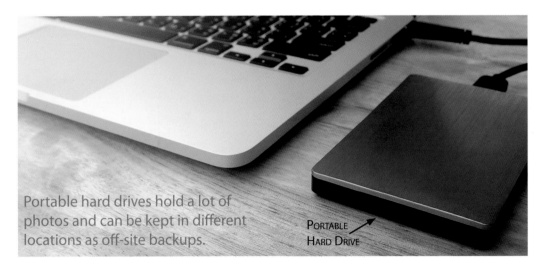

Portable hard drives hold a lot of photos and can be kept in different locations as off-site backups.

PORTABLE HARD DRIVE

A USB flash drive is an easy and portable way to back up your photographs. It is a good device to use when traveling.

If you're just starting out, you don't need to rent a safe deposit box. Store your off-site backup at a friend or relative's house for safekeeping. You'll be glad you did if your files are ever damaged.

Some photographers store off-site backups in the Cloud. That means using the Internet to automatically store digital copies on large computer servers run by companies such as Dropbox, Apple, or Google. Cloud storage can be impractical because digital photo collections often grow to many gigabytes in size and could take days to upload. However, technology changes rapidly, and Cloud storage becomes more appealing with each passing year.

For extra protection, you can also keep your best files backed up on USB flash drives. After copying, toss them in a desk drawer. It's probably not totally necessary, but it'll give you peace of mind.

COPYRIGHT

Who owns your photos? You do, of course. The moment you press the shutter release button, you own the copyright to that image. To get even more protection, you can register your photos for a fee with the U.S. Copyright Office in Washington, DC, at copyright.gov. Registered or not, nobody has the right to use your images without your permission.

Copyright.gov   About Us   News

Register
Register a Copyright

GLOSSARY

APERTURE
The opening in the lens that lets light pass through to the image sensor. The aperture is usually adjustable, and measured in f-stops.

CROPPING
Using image enhancement software in the digital darkroom to eliminate unwanted portions of an image, leaving only the most important part of the scene. Cropping is a powerful way to focus attention on your subject.

DEPTH OF FIELD
A range of distance (depth), from back to front, that is in sharp focus in your scene. A "shallow" depth of field has a very narrow range of sharp focus. It is seen most often with telephoto lenses when using large apertures (such as f/2.8), and is a useful technique for blurring distracting background clutter from your images.

DIGITAL NOISE
Noise is a collection of digital artifacts, which look like clumps of grains of sand that aren't really part of the scene. It occurs most often in low-light situations where the camera sensor is set with a high ISO number.

DIGITAL SINGLE LENS REFLEX (DSLR)
A digital single lens reflex camera is a kind of camera that features interchangeable lenses and sophisticated electronics. It captures images on a digital image sensor instead of film.

F-STOP
A number that is used to tell the size of a lens's opening, or aperture. Small numbers, such as f/2.8, represent a large aperture. Small apertures, which let in less light, include f/16 and f/22.

IMAGE SENSOR

The electronic device inside a digital camera that converts light into electronic signals, which are then processed and stored on a memory card.

ISO NUMBER

A number that describes a camera sensor's sensitivity to light. Cameras that can shoot with high ISO numbers can capture images in very dim lighting conditions. The name ISO is the abbreviation for the International Organization for Standardization, a Swiss company. ISO is not an acronym for the company name. It is the root of the Greek word *isos*, which means "equal." It is pronounced "EYE-so."

MANUAL MODE

An exposure setting that lets the photographer choose both the shutter speed and the lens aperture. Today's DSLRs have extremely accurate built-in light meters. Manual mode today is used in special circumstances where control is needed, such as shooting scenes at night.

MEMORY CARD

After an image has been captured and processed by a digital camera, it is stored on a memory card, which is a solid-state storage device similar to a USB flash drive. Memory cards come in various speeds and storage capacities. Many can hold hundreds of images.

ONLINE RESOURCES

Booklinks
NONFICTION NETWORK
FREE! ONLINE NONFICTION RESOURCES

To learn more about portrait photography, visit abdobooklinks.com. These links are routinely monitored and updated to provide the most current information available.

INDEX